SMALL FURRY ANIMALS

Bat

SMALL FURRY ANIMALS

Bat

Ting Morris

Illustrated by Graham Rosewarne

W
FRANKLIN WATTS
LONDON•SYDNEY

It's early evening and you're standing outside your friend's house, waiting for her to answer the door. Suddenly the sky is full of small, winged creatures. They look like black dots, and some are flying just above the ground.

Who are these evening visitors,
and where have they come from?

Turn the page and take a closer look.

Can you keep a secret? A colony of bats lives under this roof, but you're probably the first person to have spotted the tiny tenants. They sleep during the day and leave their roost only when it's dark. These bats are called pipistrelles. The ones you see are all females, and they've gathered here to have their young. Soon this small space will be packed with baby bats.

WINGED MAMMALS

Like humans, bats are mammals. A mammal has hair or fur on its body, and baby mammals are fed with milk from their mother. But bats are different from all other mammals – they can fly!

City-dwellers

Pipistrelles sometimes live in the country, but they like it best in towns and cities. They squeeze through narrow cracks to roost behind hanging tiles, loose window frames or in hollow walls, where they form colonies of 200 or more. In North America, many eastern pipistrelles live in woodlands, while western pipistrelles like buildings.

Bats around the world

There are more than 950 different kinds of bats. They live all over the world, except in icy polar regions, but most live in tropical countries. Bats are social animals and live in colonies in sheltered places such as caves, mines, hollow trees and buildings. They are night creatures and sleep during the day. When bats rest, they hang upside down.

W ho would have thought that so many bats could squeeze into such a tiny space? The whole swarm is flying off into the night. After resting all day, they are hungry and eager to stretch their wings. They are insect-eaters, but they don't hunt together – each bat has its own favourite feeding place. On warm summer nights, there are plenty of mosquitoes about.

SPEED RECORD

Red bats are the fastest bat flyers. They can reach speeds of more than 60 kilometres per hour. That's very fast – the average speed for bats is about 10 kilometres per hour.

Flying machine

A bat's mouse-like body forms the framework for a living flying machine. Its arms bend at the elbow and end in long, thin fingers that form the wings. A fine, almost hairless, double layer of skin, called a membrane, covers the arm and all the fingers. The finger bones are like the spokes of an umbrella and support the wing.

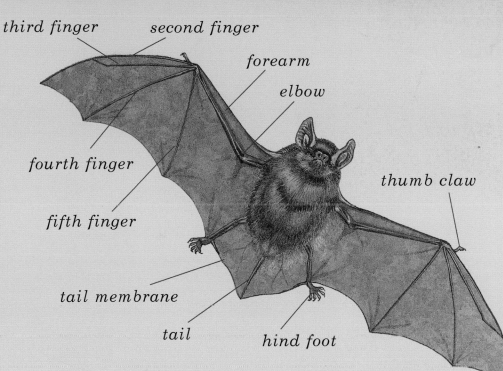

third finger

second finger

forearm

elbow

fourth finger

thumb claw

fifth finger

tail membrane

tail

hind foot

turning

twisting

on short, wide wings

Flying with their fingers

To fly, a bat stretches out its arms and fingers, and the skin unfolds and becomes tight. For turns and landings, bats change the shape of their wings by moving their fingers. Speed depends on the length of a bat's wings. Bats with long, narrow wings can fly the fastest. Short, wide wings are good for hovering in place or turning in small spaces.

flying fast

on long, narrow wings

Look at this bat as she hunts. She is flying fast, twisting and turning as she skims over the water. She picks flies off reeds and takes in mouthfuls of insects as she zooms along. Why stop when you can have an in-flight meal?

But how does she find food in the dark? And why doesn't she ever bump into anything? The reason is that bats 'see' with their ears! They make little squeaks that are too high-pitched for humans to hear. The squeaks echo off objects and tell bats what is around them.

Echolocation – seeing with ears

Bats have very good hearing (most of them have big ears) and can detect high-pitched sounds that we cannot hear. The echoes of their own squeaks tell them the shape of an object and how far away it is. This method of 'seeing' what is around them is called echolocation.

1. The bat sends out ultrasonic squeaks.

2. The squeaks bounce back from objects in the bat's flight path and into its ears.

3. The hunter homes in on the object if it's a tasty insect.

pinna

tragus

All ears

All bats have a large ear flap, called a pinna. Most insect-eating bats have a fleshy spike or earlet, called a tragus, which helps them to hear even better.

Bat talk

Brown bats open their mouths to send out sounds. Horseshoe bats send ultrasonic squeaks through their noses.

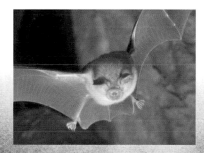

horseshoe bat

little brown bat

The little gap under the roof has turned into a busy nursery. During the warm summer months, bats give birth to their young. When a baby is born, its mother makes a cradle with her wings and suckles it. Her pink baby is blind and hairless, but it has strong claws. It clings tightly to its mother, and she feeds and grooms her baby night and day.

Most bats have one baby, but sometimes they have two. Can you spot twins in the roost?

Bat babies

Newborn bats are blind, but they have strong claws and milk teeth. A baby bat drinks its mother's rich milk every few hours, which makes it grow very quickly. Within a few days, the young bats open their eyes and are able to hang on their own. At three weeks of age, a baby bat is almost fully grown and can fly.

THE NURSERY ROOST

In the winter, male and female bats share the same roost. But when the weather starts to warm up, the colony splits up, and the females set up a nursery roost in a ready-made warm space in a tree, cave or attic. Bats stay close together to keep warm, and usually all of the mothers in the roost have their babies at the same time.

Keeping clean

Bats spend a long time grooming themselves and their babies. They hang by one foot and use their tongue and the other foot for cleaning the fur. The thumb claw makes a good comb. The wings need extra care, and oils made in the bat's glands keep them smooth.

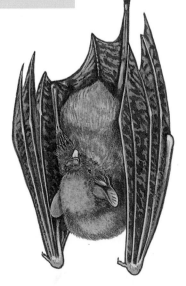

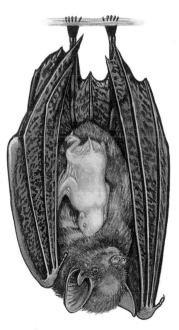

If you looked out now, you would see the group flying off again. But tonight the bats are carrying their young. Each baby clings tightly to its mother's fur. The youngsters are quite heavy now, but they still can't fly on their own. So why are the mothers taking them on this night flight, rather than leaving them in the roost as usual? Perhaps the bats sense danger.

14

ON THE MOVE

Bats often move roost several times during the summer. They know a number of places, usually south-facing, to which they return every year. But if the weather turns cold or the roost is disturbed, the colony quickly moves out.

Cry-babies

You might wonder how bat mothers can find their own baby in this cluster. The answer is that baby bats cry for their mother with high-pitched calls. Each mother knows her own baby's special squeak and smell.

Flying with mother

During the night, mother bats fly out for quick snacks between frequent suckling. Some bats always carry their young with them, even on their nightly flights for food. Fruit bat mothers carry their young with them until they are eight weeks old. Pipistrelle mothers usually leave their babies in the nursery, huddled together for warmth.

Now that the young bats are three weeks old, they go out on short flights under their mother's wing. The youngsters are not afraid of flying, but there are many dangers lurking outside the nursery. You are not the only one watching the roost. A cat has noticed when the bats come out to feed, and it's waiting on the roof now, ready to pounce. Baby bats are an easy catch and make a tasty meal.

First flight

Young pipistrelles make their first flight when they are three weeks old. Their mothers still feed and groom them and, on their nightly outings, they receive lessons on catching insects. By six weeks of age, the young bats can look after themselves, and the nursery colony splits up.

Enemies

Bats don't have many enemies, because they are hidden during the day and can fly away from other animals at night. Dusk is the most dangerous time, when owls and cats watch for them as they leave the roost. But people are bats' greatest enemies. Pesticides kill the insects bats feed on and sometimes poison the bats too. In Asia, some people hunt fruit bats. In many countries, laws now protect bats.

SUPERSTITIONS

Bats have strange faces and can seem frightening. Some people used to think that witches turned themselves into bats, but in China bats are symbols of long life and happiness. Most bats are harmless.

WHERE'S THE CATCH?

Instead of using their fingers, which are needed for flying, some insect-eating bats catch their prey in their big tail flap. This works like a fishing net. While still flying, the bat picks the insect out of its tail.

While female bats are looking after their babies, the males stay together in small groups. They have many summer roosts, and some don't even join a colony. Hunting for food is all a male does, but it keeps him busy after dark. This male pipistrelle has caught a big moth and is munching on it in comfort – upside down, of course!

Mayfly

Midge

Caddis fly

Mosquito

Pipistrelle special

Pipistrelles hunt over water, along hedgerows, and in woods, parks and gardens. They eat for a couple of hours and then hang to digest their meal. They swallow whole swarms of midges and gnats as they fly along. Bats drink by skimming their tongue on the surface of a pond or river.

Moth

Lacewing

Different tastes

Some bats eat frogs and fish. The Australian ghost bat hunts birds and small mammals, including other bats. Vampire bats of South America drink blood from cows, pigs, goats and horses. On a liquid diet of blood, this bat needs only two razor-sharp front teeth to shave away its victim's fur and bite. It then laps up the blood through a groove in its lower lip.

It's autumn, and the male bats are calling for a mate. Although these squeaks are not as high-pitched as the bats' hunting cries, they are still too high for people to hear. But a passing female understands the male's call and recognizes his special smell.

Can you see the two bats high in the tree?

MATING

Bats mate in the autumn, when males and females find each other by their calls and a smell made in special glands in the skin. Males call out as they fly around, or hang in a roosting place where they can be visited by female bats.

A long wait

After mating, the female bat carries the male's sperm in her body until the next spring before she gives birth. She sleeps through the winter, and fertilization takes place when it is warm enough for the baby to grow inside her. Pipistrelles are pregnant for about 44 days, or longer in cold weather.

Noisy chorus

Groups of African hammer-headed fruit bats gather in trees and call for hours at mating time. When a female comes near, each hammerhead tries to impress her by being the noisiest of the group.

WINTER ROOST

A bat's winter roost is called a hibernaculum. Cool and damp places, such as caves and mines, are ideal. There the hibernating bat's temperature drops to that of its surroundings. It goes cold and stiff and does not need to eat or drink.

The nights are chilly now, and there is less food available. A busy bat needs to eat hundreds or thousands of insects a night to stay alive. Some kinds of bats fly away to warmer places, but pipistrelles sleep through the winter. Before they go to sleep, though, they must put on lots of extra fat. Males and females come together at this time to find a safe winter roost. Watch them as they move into their winter quarters – you won't see them again until next spring.

Cave news

Caves offer perfect roosts for bats, where they can nurse their young or hibernate safely and undisturbed. Around 100 million Mexican free tailed bats roost in the Carlsbad Caverns of New Mexico. There are so many that they blacken the sky when they leave the caves.

Inside a bat's cave

Many caves in Central and South America house different kinds of bats. Each species makes its home in a part of the cave that suits it best. Big-eared bats live close to the entrance. Moustached bats hang deep in the darkness. In large caves, many bats cling to stalactites or shelter in cracks in the ground.

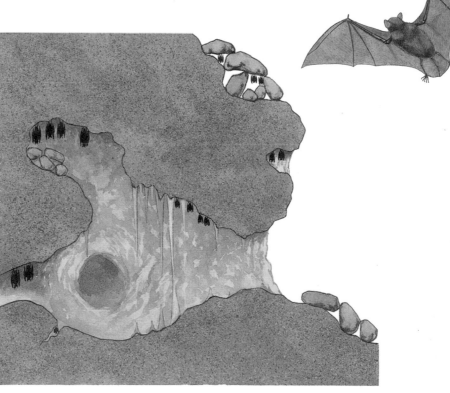

23

HIBERNATION

Hibernation is a deep sleep that lasts through the winter. Bats that live in cold places hibernate when there is not enough food available. Before they go into hibernation, they store up spare fat to see them through the coming months.

For four cold winter months, the bats have been hanging here without moving. They look frozen, but they are alive and well. It's getting warmer every day, and soon they will start waking up from their long sleep, or hibernation. Then they'll be very hungry, and who wouldn't be after such a long time? But it will take a while for them to warm up and get their wings working. So keep an eye on that bell tower, because soon they'll be flying out and the sky will again be full of small, winged creatures.

Biggest and smallest

The largest bats are the fruit-eating flying foxes. Most live in Africa and the Pacific islands, and some weigh more than 1 kilogram. The greater fruit bat is the biggest. Its body is up to 45 centimetres long, with a wingspan of 1.5 metres.

The smallest bat is the Kitti's hog-nosed bat of Thailand. At 2.5 centimetres long, and with a weight of just 2 grams, it is no bigger than a bumblebee!

Tent makers

Some tropical bats nibble a large palm leaf into a tent shape and camp out underneath.

Branching out

Bats that live in warm climates don't need to hibernate. Most flying foxes hang in large groups from the upper branches of trees. Thousands of greater fruit bats roost during the day and fly off in search of fruit when it gets dark.

Males and females
hibernate in winter roosts.

Bats usually
mate in
the autumn.

BAT
CIRCLE OF LIFE

Young bats eat a lot
during autumn. They
are fully grown by
the autumn of their
second year.

In the spring, female bats form colonies. They set up nursery roosts and give birth in the summer.

Youngsters start to fly when they are three weeks old, following their mother and learning to catch insects.

Young bats are weaned when they are six weeks old. The nursery colony then splits up.

Glossary

colony A large group of animals that live close together as a community.

glands Organs inside the body that produce important substances.

groom To clean the fur or skin.

hibernate To sleep through the winter.

hover To stay in one place in the air.

mate When a male and female animal come together to make young.

mosquitoes Small, biting insects.

nursery A place where young animals are cared for.

pregnant With young developing inside the body.

roost A place where bats rest and sleep.

social animals Animals that like to live together in groups.

sperm Fluid produced by male animals that makes a female's eggs grow into babies.

suckle To feed milk to a young animal.

swarm A large number of animals that stay close to each other and move around together.

ultrasonic Referring to sounds that are so high-pitched that humans cannot hear them.

weaned No longer drinking its mother's milk.

wingspan The distance from the tip of one outstretched wing to the other.

INDEX